Windows 8 User's Manual

A Complete Guide to Use Windows 8 like a Professional

Disclaimer

The author has tried to be an authentic source of the information provided in this report. However, the author does not oppose the additional information available over the internet in an updated form. All guidelines presented in this publication are available to educate readers only. The information included in this book cannot be compared with the guidelines provided with Windows 8. All readers can seek help from skilled professionals for further advice.

Ignoring any of the guidelines and misusing the software may cause damage to it. Therefore, the author is not responsible for commercial or personal damage caused by readers.

Contents

Disclaimer..2

Why Read This Manual Before Using Windows 8?...5

If you are like many others who want to stay updated with the latest technologies, and want to adapt the same as soon as it is possible for you, then Windows 8 is for you! However, it is important to know that this version differs a lot from the earlier versions developed by Microsoft. This makes it necessary to learn all the new features of Windows 8 before using it in your tablet....................................5

Introduction to Windows 8 6

What Is So Good About Windows 8?...9

New Features 11

The Lock Screen 11

The "Start" Screen 13

The Freedom to Organize Tiles 15

Using the "Start" button in Windows 8 27

The Touch Hardware 28

Getting Used to the Touch Experience 28

Using Keyboard and Mouse: Shortcuts You Can Use 32

Keyboard Shortcuts...32

Windows + X 49

Ctrl + Alt + Delete 52

Mouse Shortcuts...67

Security and Safety 76

"Windows Store" Apps..78

Web Browsers...79

Desktop and Interface 80

Secure Boot..81

Removed Features 82

Start Button and Start Menu 82

Windows Aero 83

Boot-to-Desktop...83

Desktop Notifications 84

Windows Media Center 85

Previous Versions 85

DVD Playback 87

Hardware Requirements.. 88

Tips for Upgradation 91

Windows 8 in Different Editions 94

Windows 8 Pro... 94

Windows 8 Enterprise... 95

Final Word... 97

Why Read This Manual Before Using Windows 8?

If you are like many others who want to stay updated with the latest technologies, and want to adapt the same as soon as it is possible for you, then Windows 8 is for you! However, it is important to know that this version differs a lot from the earlier versions developed by Microsoft. This makes it necessary to learn all the new features of Windows 8 before using it in your tablet.

Along with many new features introduced in Windows 8, a few of them are replaced by advanced features to provide a better user-experience to all tablet and PC users. Keeping this in consideration, the main challenge is to learn every bit of those features, so that you can have excellent command over them while using Windows 8. This guide has been designed to fulfill the same purpose.

Throughout the book, you will find each new feature of Windows 8, along with many other important details you should know about Windows 8 before actually using it. Once you are done with reading this manual, you will be able to use Windows 8 proficiently.

Introduction to Windows 8

Developed by Microsoft, Windows 8 is Microsoft Windows' latest version. It has been developed for multiple platforms such as, desktops, tablets, home theater personal computers, and laptops.

Though Windows 7 entered the market in 2009, the developers of Windows began working on Windows 8 before the launch of Windows 7.

The release of Windows 8 has introduced significant changes in terms of using computers in a modernized way. This new version of Microsoft is focused towards enhancing the user experience on tablets. The aim is to compete with Apple's IOS and Android in a better way.

Windows 8

Meet the new Windows

Windows 8 has been re-imagined to focus on your life. The beautiful, fast, and fluid design is perfect for a range of hardware: tablets, laptops and PCs.

Among many new features, some of the most prominent ones included in Windows 8 include its new "touch user interface", and a new "Start screen" that shows the grid of updating tiles. These tiles represent applications. This start screen has replaced the "Start menu", that was included in the previous versions of Windows.

Furthermore, its new "app" platform emphasizes on its touch screen input while the new "Windows Store" is used to purchase applications, so that the applications can be run on this operating system.

Unlike earlier versions of Windows, Windows 8 has taken advantage of the emerging technologies such as, USB 3.0, ARM architecture, 4Kn Advanced Format, and cloud computing. All this included in this version of Windows makes it worth using, especially for those who are early adaptors of latest technologies.

What Is So Good About Windows 8?

Every time a new version of Microsoft Windows enters the market, it brings a lot of curiosity. "What does the newer version of Windows actually offers me?" is a common question running in each user's mind. However, when it comes to analyzing the functionality and new features of Windows 8, there is a lot more to expect and explore! So, what makes Windows 8 so unique?

Microsoft has envisioned its operating system that has high usability, starting from keyboard less tablets to gigantic servers that are running numerous processors at a time.

Though Windows 8 had been in the initial phase of development before releasing Windows 7, Microsoft came to the conclusion that the newer version required some more time, till the concept of using tablet computers becomes common.

Now that using tablets is as common as using mobile phones, it is time to delight the relevant users with the launch of Windows 8. This way, Microsoft has targeted the right segment of computer users by developing Windows 8 for them. With enhanced features and increased visibility of each and every application, Microsoft expects to see a higher level of adaption of this version among home-based as well as business-oriented computer users.

New Features

The Lock Screen

As soon as you switch on your tablet, the first thing you will notice in your recently installed Windows 8 will be the lock screen. This screen is entirely different from the lock screen you normally see in other Windows devices. Though the lock screen in your previous Windows gave you updates about date and time, along with the displayed background, what Windows 8 offers you is something unique, i.e. Picture Password.

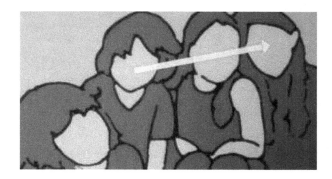

Picture Password represents a specific digital image or photo. If you know what type of combination to draw on this image, you will be able to unlock the screen. Drawing the right combination of lines or shapes on this image is all you are required to do. Once this is done, you will log in to Windows 8.

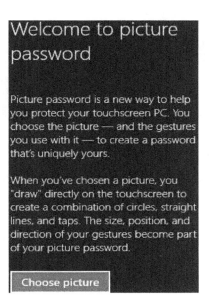

Lines and circles are the most common passwords you can use to unlock the screen of your tablet. Choose your own drawing sign to get access to this. For instance, you can draw a hat on the squirrel.

Setting up a password picture depends on you. This means that you can choose a picture according to your own choice.

However, before stepping ahead, you will be asked to set the gestures in the image. This way, you will be able to choose a password that is easy for you to unlock the screen.

The "Start" Screen

When you are done with setting up a picture password, the next thing you will come across is the Start screen, the most frequently visited place in your PC.

You will be coming back to this screen every now and then, especially when you need to choose an app or other features of Windows 8. The look of the Start screen will give you an experience that is quite similar to that of Windows Phone. This is mainly because you can see "tiles" representing each app individually.

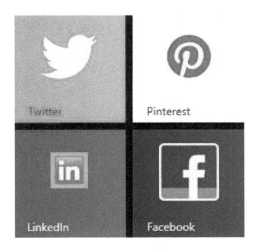

What makes the Start screen unique is the fact that each tile shows various actions, revealing what is inside the app.

For instance, if you want to activate a social media app, you can get an idea of the social networking updates by simply going to the start screen. The tile of the app will show you the news feed. If you are interested to open the app, all you need to do is to tap the tile.

The Freedom to Organize Tiles

Windows 8 offers you an enhanced sense of personalization. Now, you can customize the tiles of your apps, making them more accessible for you, even if they are on the start screen. So, it is time to organize the tiles of apps according to your own choice!

There are various options available for this. For instance, you can select the tile size that provides a better user interface. Furthermore, you can also choose from live tiles or static tiles, and arrange them into groups.

If you do not want a specific tile, you can remove it from the Start screen. Do you want it again? You can add it back anytime!

Tiles and their Types

On the start screen, you can see the tiles that represent the apps you have installed. You will come across two types of tiles:

Metro Apps

Metro apps are the apps with custom-designed tiles. These tiles do not include only the name of a particular app and its icon, but represents the overall image of the app on the start screen of Windows 8. This enables you to see the variety of images on the tile of the app, which have been specifically developed to enhance the Windows 8 user interface.

Non-Metro Apps

Non-metro apps are those with standard icon and the app names. You can identify this easily when you have customized the tiles. These tiles are in the form of squares only, showing the name of the app, along with the logo, such as that of Google Chrome.

Selecting Tiles

If you want to customize tiles of your apps to make the start screen more organized, you are required to select the tiles first. To do this, right-click the tiles you want to customize. When you do this, the tile will be selected. At the same time, you will see a bar popping up on the screen, providing you all the options available for the next move.

In this step, it is important to know that Windows 8 will not give the same options for all types of tiles. This indicates that you will have to choose an option according to the tile you want to customize. So, look for the options first.

If you want to select a multiple number of tiles, you can do this by right-clicking on them. When you are done with selecting more than one tile, you will get some different options to continue with your customization. However, keep in mind that the operations to be performed on the selected tiles depend on which tiles you have chosen to customize.

Deselecting a tile is as simple as selecting it. To deselect, just right-click on the tile again, and you are done.

Available Actions

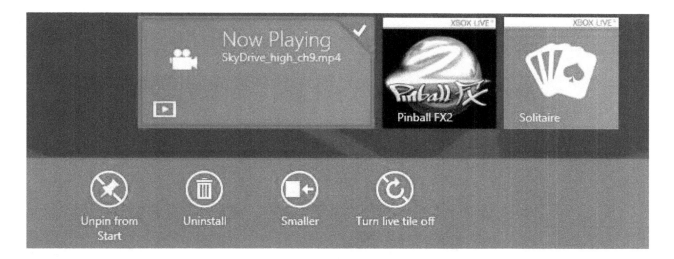

When you have selected the app tiles, some actions will become available to you. Again, this actually depends on which type of tile you have selected. For instance, if you have selected Metro apps, your actions will be limited to unpinning, selecting the live tile "on/off", uninstalling, and choosing a smaller or larger size.

However, it is not necessary that all Metro apps have the option of choosing a different size available.

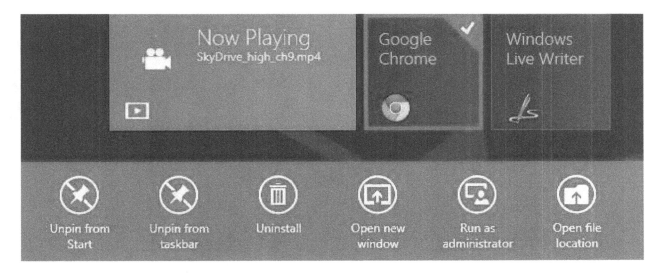

Likewise, non-Metro apps will provide you almost the same options for customization. This type of tiles enables you to choose unpinning, uninstallation, pinning the non-Metro app to your taskbar, starting new window, running an app and using it as administrator, and opening the file location.

Removing (Unpinning) Tiles

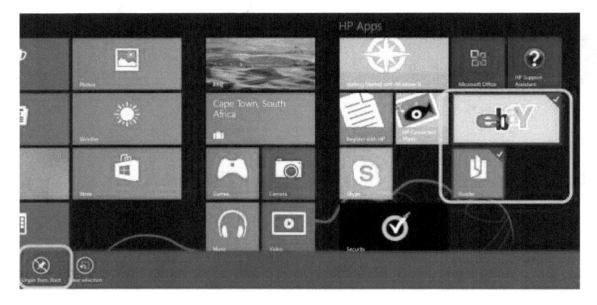

The process of removing tiles from the start screen requires you to select the tile you want to unpin. Once you are done with this, you will see the option, "Unpin from Start." Click on this option, and the tile of the selected app will be removed from your start screen.

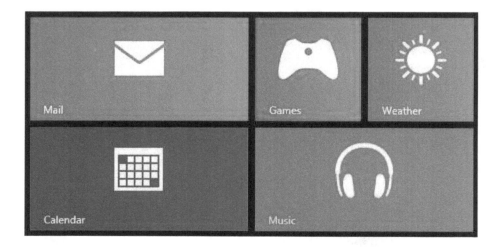

However, doing this does not mean that the program has been uninstalled. In other words, you have removed it from the main screen of your Windows 8 tablet only. So, if you want to add the same tile again to your start screen, you can do this easily.

Adding (Unpinning) Tiles

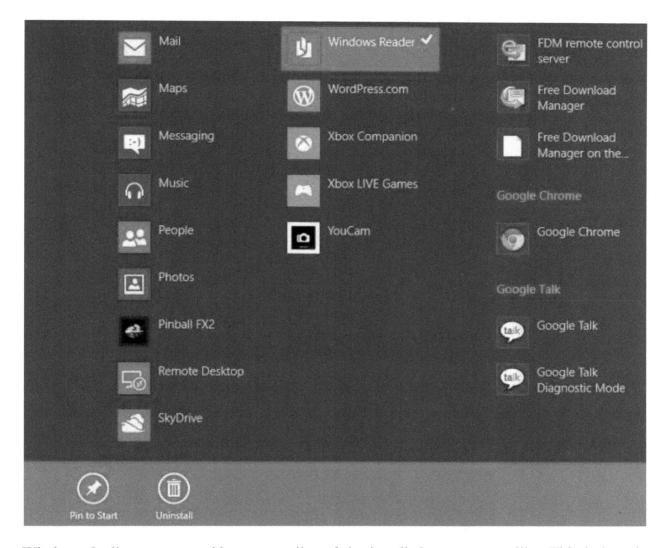

Windows 8 allows you to add as many tiles of the installed apps as you like. This is how it provides a better user experience to its users. Change the way you get access to your apps and make it easier. Simply pin the tiles on the start screen by learning the procedure once.

To pin tiles, right-click on the Start screen's background. Make sure you do not right-click on the tile itself. Once you have done this, an "All apps" button will appear on the screen. Click on this button. You will get a list of the apps you installed.

Now, right-click on the app you want to pin. You will get an option, "Pin to Start" on the Start screen. Click it and you are done!

Resizing Tiles

It is best for you to resize the tiles of your installed apps if you want many of them to be visible on your Start screen. Make this possible by selecting the tile to be resized first. Right-clicking it will give you the resizing option. This will also depend on the current size of the tile.

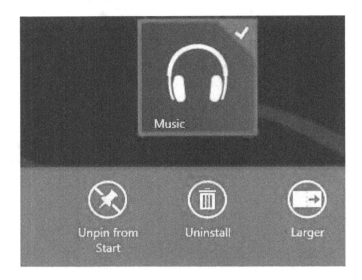

The above image shows a tile with a smaller size. For this reason, Windows 8 gives the "Larger" option. Now, see the below-mentioned image. The tile has a large and rectangular size. Therefore, you are required to resize by clicking on the "smaller option."

Whatever the current size is, Windows 8 will identify it for you. So, you just need to click on the given option. The tile will be resized.

Organizing Windows Tiles in Categories/Groups

It makes a lot of sense to arrange the installed app tiles into relevant sections. This is definitely a great way to select an app without searching for it for too long. Secondly, the new feature of organizing app tiles provided by Windows 8 will help you keep all the similar apps together.

To get all your apps in appropriate sections, simply drag the chosen tiles and drop them from one place to the start screen. They will automatically snap evenly to the Start screen grid. This way, all the related apps will be aligned well to the grid.

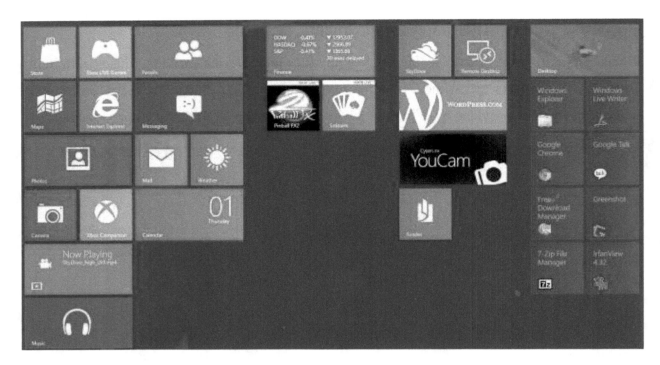

Another thing to do is to move the installed apps into various columns, along with giving some space between each adjacent column. Simply drag a tile on the gray bar. Doing this will give the tile its own column. Once you have made the column, you can classify other tiles into these columns accordingly, making a separate group for each.

Customized Tiles: The Final Look

Once you have customized the tiles of your apps successfully on the start screen, you will get a look similar to the one portrayed in the following image:

If your apps are organized the same way, then you can benefit from this customization style of Windows 8. In addition, this will not only help you stay organized with your daily schedule, it will also allow you to save a lot of time.

Organizer

Getting everything related to your daily tasks such as, calendar, weather updates, mail, and people helps you stay in touch with everyone, along with meeting critical deadlines.

Web

Are you planning to shop for something after reading the product reviews? Windows 8 will make this easy for you with everything organized in a single group.

Media

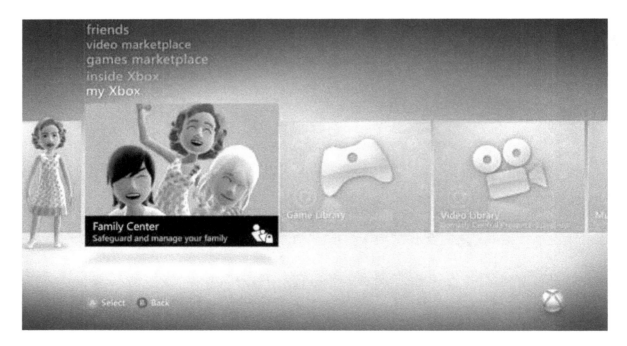

Whether you like to take photos or are interested in music, you can do all this in your start screen.

Using the "Start" button in Windows 8

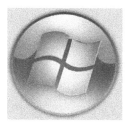

Can't work with the "Start screen" of Windows 8 as comfortable as you used to with the "Start button" offered in the earlier version of Windows? There is nothing to worry about. You can get the same user experience in Windows 8 as well.

The process is quite easy. All you need to do is to install an app that has been specifically designed to serve this purpose. For example, you can install an app called Classic Shell. Along with removing Windows 8 Start screen and bringing the Start button back, it will help you get back the options which were available in the earlier versions of Windows. Another option is to download the Start button from a credible website.

The Touch Hardware

Introducing the touch experience, Windows 8 also educates those who are using the touch interface for the first time. Swiping through the screen is definitely a new approach, which was not available in Microsoft's previous Windows.

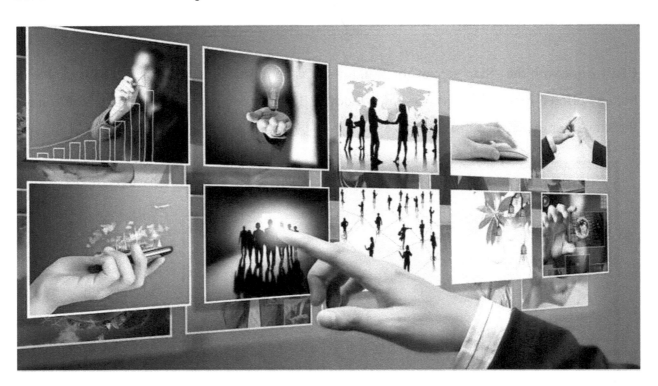

Getting Used to the Touch Experience

The touch interactions you can learn while using Windows 8 are explained in detail. Follow each step to get excellent command over your touch screen.

Know About Any Program

The procedure is quite simple. If you see a program which is unfamiliar to you, simply press the icon, and hold your finger to learn about its functionality. Its drop-down menu gives additional options.

Press and hold **to learn**

Slide to Drag

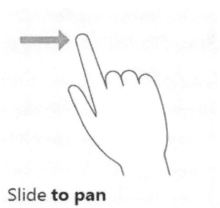

Slide **to pan**

Moving a tile from one screen to the other requires you to drag it by sliding your finger.

Tap To Open an App

Tap **for primary action**

When it comes to loading, activating, or opening an application, you need to tap on the icon itself.

Swipe to Perform Several Tasks

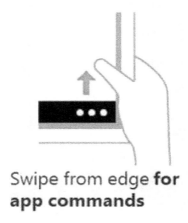

Swipe from edge **for app commands**

Swiping on the screen has a lot to do with performing various tasks simultaneously. For instance, if you want to minimize an opened app, you can do this by swiping from the top of the app to the bottom. To make the app visible on your screen again, swipe it from the bottom to the top.

Rotate According To the View

Turn **to rotate**

Sometimes you want to rotate a picture to get a better and larger view. Unlike Windows 7, this new version of Windows gives you the option to perform the task without using the mouse. So, just use your finger, and turn the picture from right to left, or from left to right in a circular motion.

Pinch Inwards and Outwards

Pinch and stretch
to zoom

Now, there is no need to adjust the size of text in while reading an important document, or following specific directions from a map. Use your fingers to get the smaller or larger view. For instance, if you want to view a document in smaller size, pinch it inwards as mentioned in the image above.

Likewise, you can enlarge the same document by stretching it outwards.

Select an App

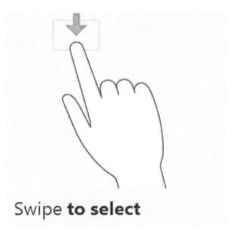

Swipe **to select**

You can select any app and choose a task by swiping the screen.

Using Keyboard and Mouse: Shortcuts You Can Use

By now, you must have got a clear idea that learning the touch screen methods is important for using Windows 8, simply because this new version of Microsoft Windows has been designed specifically as the "touch first system."

However, it is okay to use a keyboard and mouse if you are not used to working with the touch-screen technology. For this reason, Windows 8 has also introduced the use of mouse and keyboard to ease the overall user experience.

Keyboard Shortcuts

The following keyboard shortcuts are developed to make things easier for you, while enjoying the most from Windows 8:

Windows

Go to your Start Screen directly

Windows + C

Open the "Charm bar"

Windows + I

Open "Settings" from Charm bar

Common shortcuts related to Charm bars

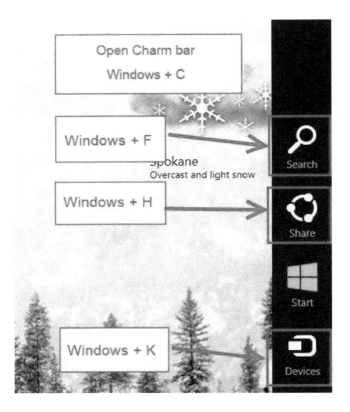

Windows + M

Minimize all opened windows

Windows + Shift + M

Restore the minimized windows

Windows + W

Search for the settings

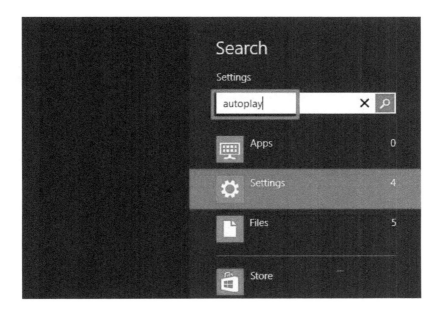

Windows + Q

Search for apps

Windows + Up Arrow

Maximize the current window.

Windows + F

Search for your files

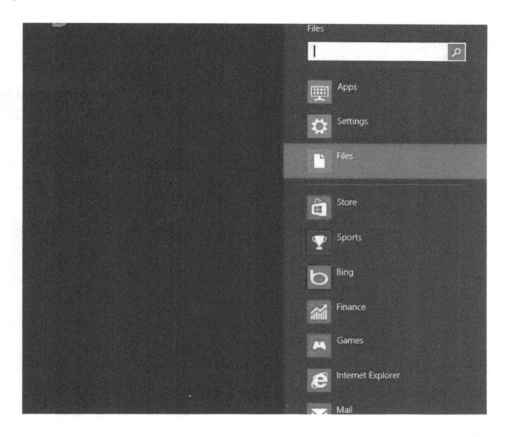

Windows + T

Cycle through various items on your taskbar.

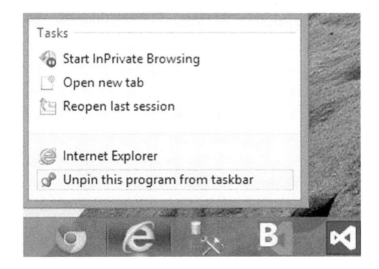

Windows + Z

Open the bar containing apps

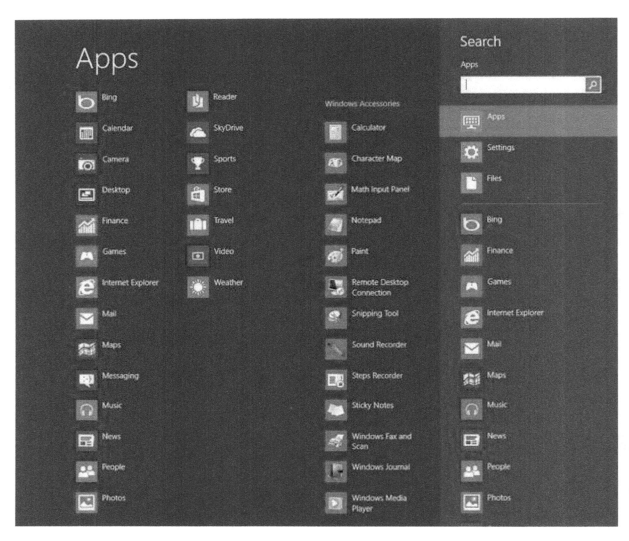

Windows + D

See the desktop

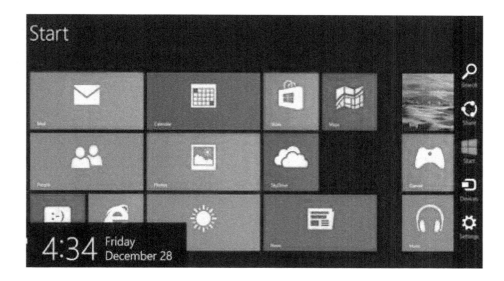

Windows + E

Start the Windows Explorer

Windows + Space

Switch keyboard layout and input language

Windows + O

Lock "device orientation"

Windows + Enter

Launch Narrator

Windows + Page Up

Shift the "metro-style" application or the start screen on your screen on the left

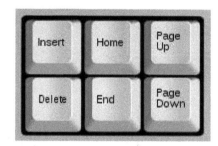

Windows + Page Down

Shift your start screen or any "metro-style" application on your screen on the right

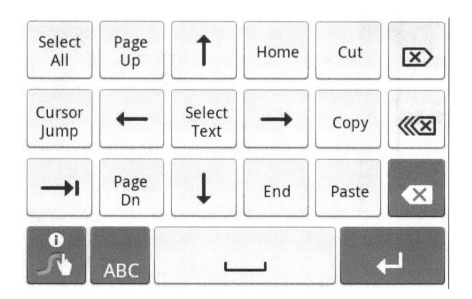

Windows + Tab

Cycle through different apps

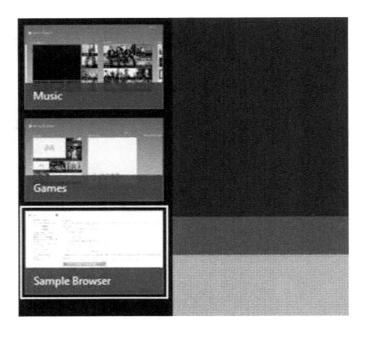

Alt + Tab

Besides switching desktop apps, the combination of Alt and Tab also applies well to apps from Windows Store. Press Alt +Tab to see all the Windows Store apps running on your system.

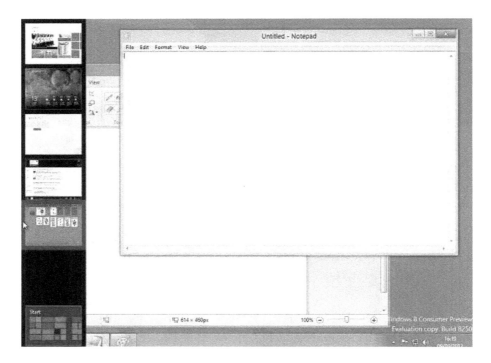

Windows + Shift + Tab

Cycle through the applications in their reverse order

Windows + Ctrl + Tab

Cycle through the apps while snapping them when cycling

Windows + /

Start "Input Method Editor (IME)" reconversion

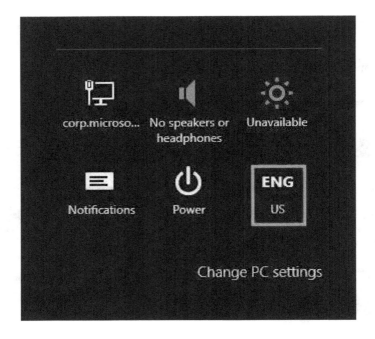

Windows + V

Windows + J

Change foreground between filled and snapped apps

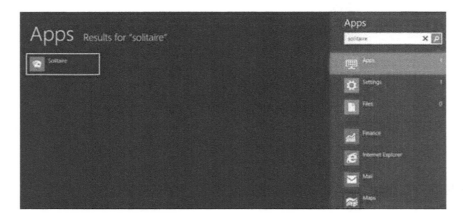

Windows + Shift

Snap any application

Windows + K

Open the "Connect" Charm

Windows + H

Open the "Share" Charm

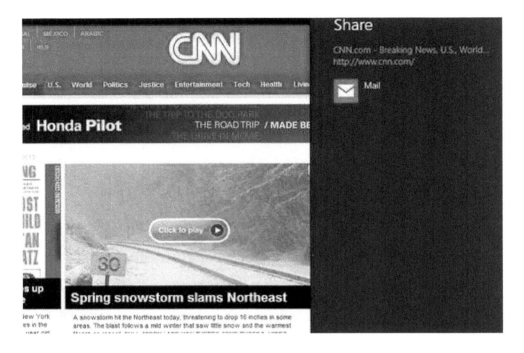

Windows + G

Cycle through "Desktop Gadgets"

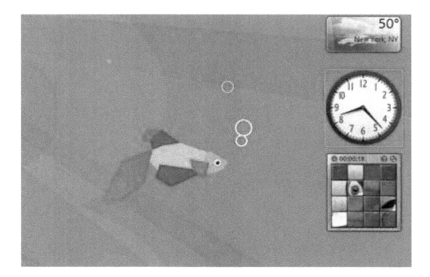

Windows + P

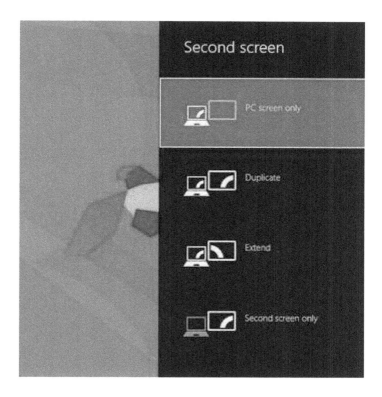

Windows + R

Run

Windows + T

Run desktop apps and set its focus on the taskbar

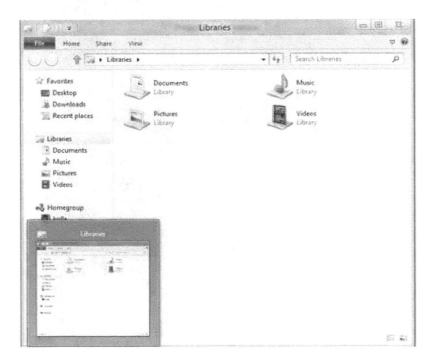

Windows + U

Get access to some common tools

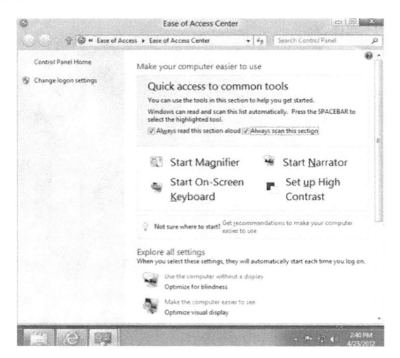

Windows + X

Get commands for using quick links.

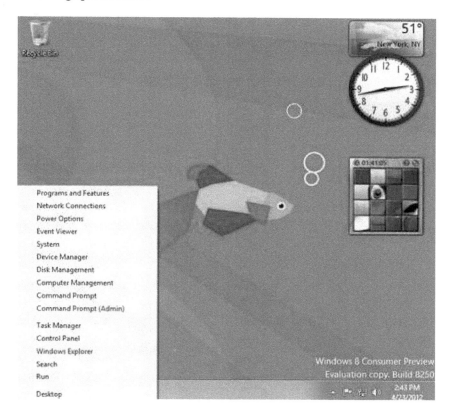

Windows +.

Run two apps simultaneously on your screen.

Ctrl + Shift + Esc

Open the Task Manager

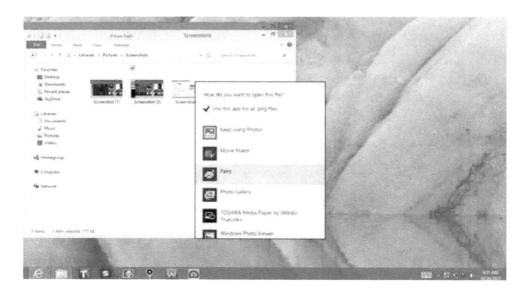

Start + Print Screen

Take screenshot. It will directly be saved in the Pictures folder.

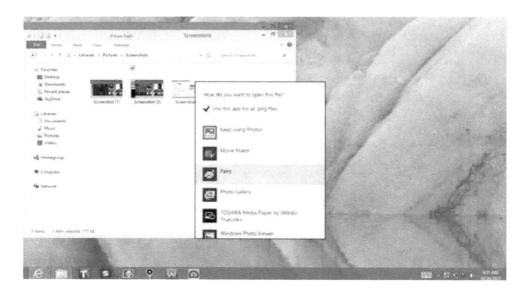

Start + Tab

Open the Multi-tasking menu

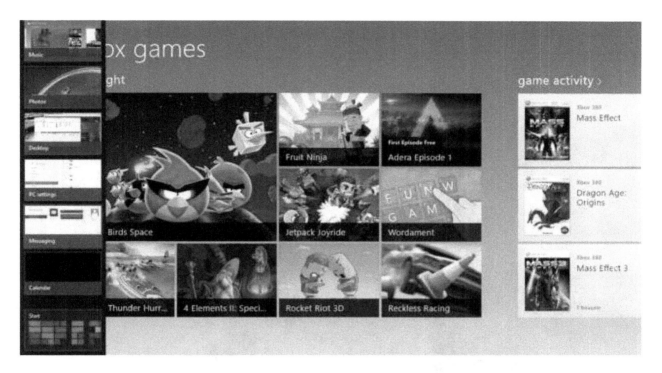

Alt + F1

Close an app directly

Ctrl + Alt + Delete

Tap the icon at the bottom-right corner of the screen. It will show you the restart, shutdown, sleep, log out, and lock options.

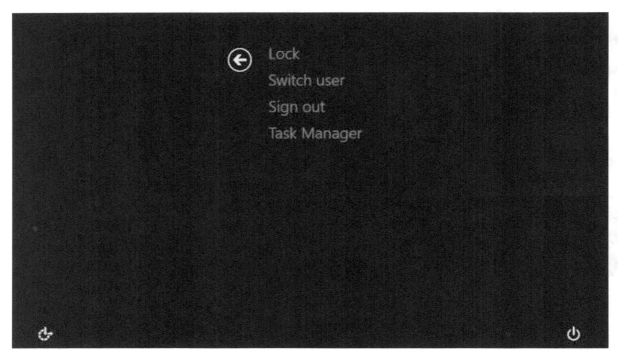

You may come across a situation in which you will need to restart your computer. Perform this task by using this shortcut immediately.

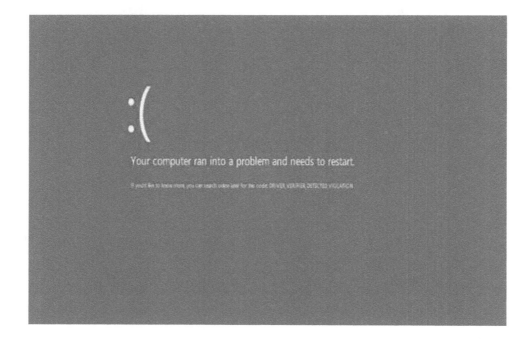

Shift + Delete

Remove any selected item without selecting the Recycle Bin.

Windows + L

Lock computer.

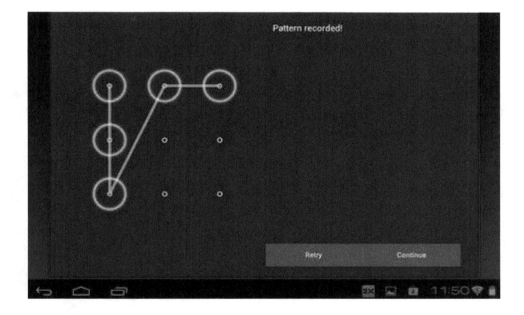

Windows + Ctrl + B

Access a program that currently displays a notification.

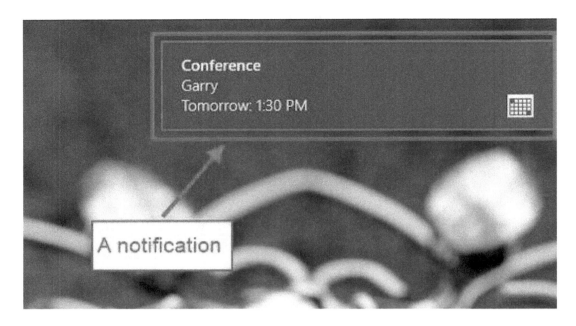

Windows + Ctrl + F

Open the dialogue box of "Find Computers."

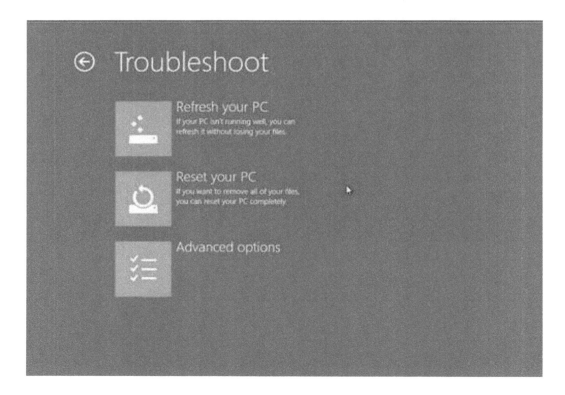

Windows + Shift + .

Shift the Windows screen split on the left side.

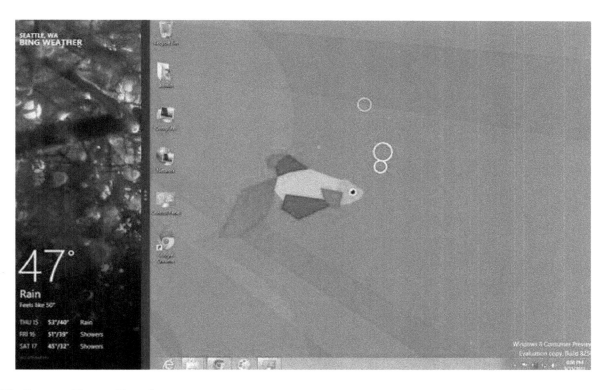

Windows + Pause/Break

Open the "System Page."

Windows + Up Arrow

Maximize the current window.

Windows + Down Arrow

Minimize or restore the current window.

Windows + Home

Minimize all the windows except your current window.

Windows + Left Arrow

Tile the window by choosing the left-side of your screen.

Windows + Right Arrow

Tile the window by choosing the right-side of your screen

Windows + F1

Launch "Windows Help and Support"

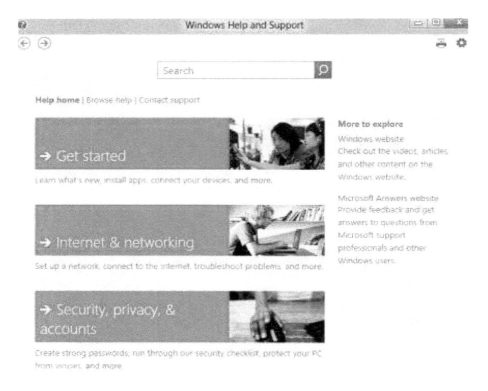

Alt

Display the Menu Bar that is hidden.

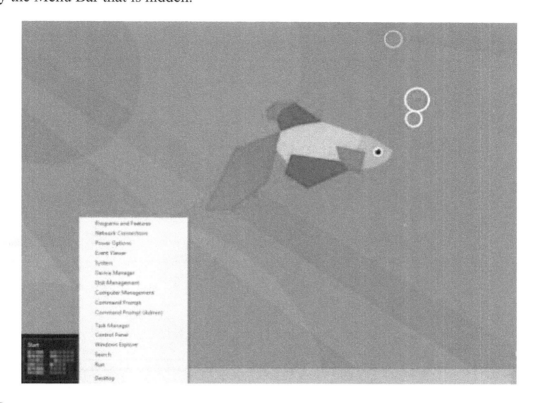

Alt + D

Select the "Address Bar"

Alt + P

Open Windows Explorer and display the "Preview Pane."

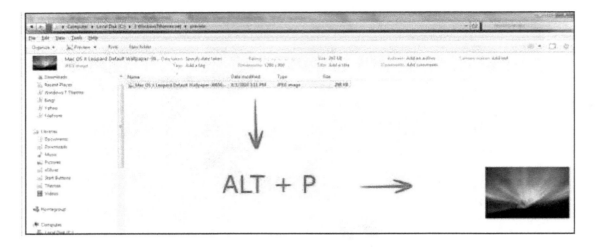

Alt + F4

Close your current window, and open the "Shut Down Windows" dialog box.

Alt + Spacebar

Get access to the "Shortcut" menu in current window.

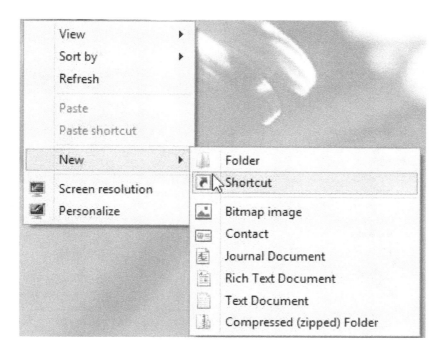

Alt + Esc

Cycle between the opened programs in the same order where these programs were opened.

Alt + Enter

Select an item and open its "Properties" dialog box.

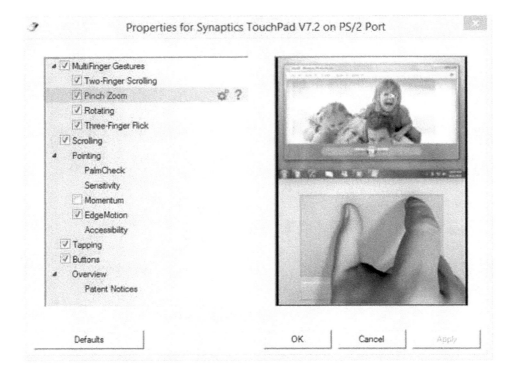

Ctrl + A

Select all the items on the screen

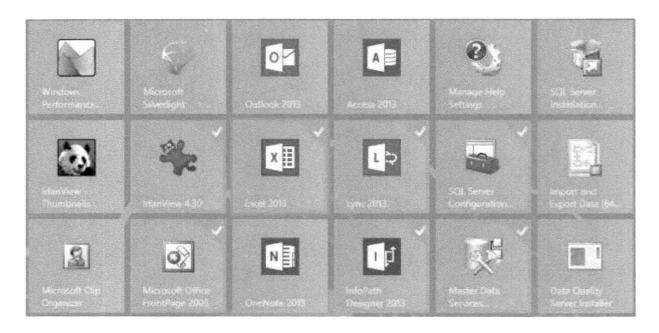

Ctrl + C

Copy a selected item.

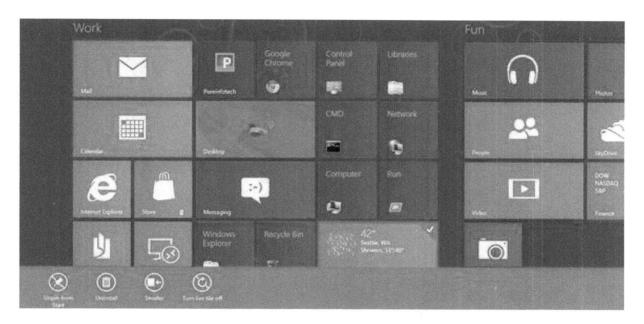

Ctrl + X

Cut a selected item.

Ctrl + V

Paste the item selected.

Ctrl + D

Delete the selected item.

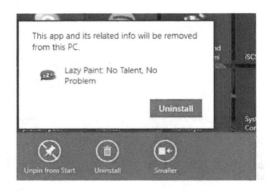

Ctrl + Z

Undo the action performed recently.

Ctrl + Y

Redo the action performed just now.

Ctrl + N

Use Windows Explorer to open new window.

Ctrl + W

Close your current window that was opened in the Windows Explorer.

Ctrl + E

Select the "Search" box located at the top right corner of your window.

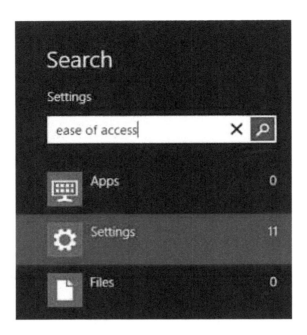

Ctrl + Shift + N

Create a new folder.

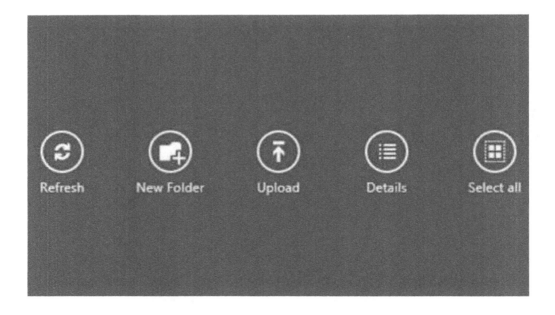

Mouse Shortcuts

If you want to use Windows 8 by using your mouse rather than the swiping option, then knowing the shortcuts will help you gain a good user experience.

Start off by learning where the hotspots of the main screen are, and when you should actually right-click them.

Some Basics Mouse Shortcuts:

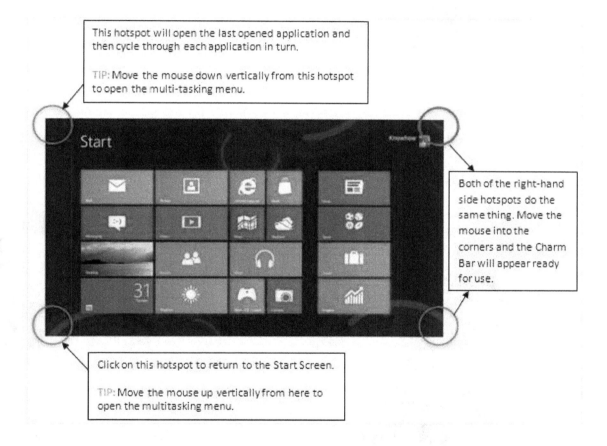

Besides following the tips mentioned in the image above, do not forget to right-click! In this situation, you should remember that the interface of Windows 8 runs in its full screen. This indicates that you will not find any drop-down menus, which is why you are required to right-click on the apps and other programs rather than clicking on them directly.

The Charms Menu

Move the mouse to the bottom or top right corner of the screen. Leave it on the same corner for a while. This will show you the Charms menu.

Switching Tasks Quickly

Move the mouse to the left edge's middle. Click it while dragging. A new app will appear. If you want to see all the other running apps, move the mouse to the bottom or top left corners on your screen. Along with this, take the cursor to the center of the screen until the apps list is disappeared.

Using 2 Apps Simultaneously

Bring two apps on your desktop, and use them simultaneously by snapping the first app to the left or right side of the screen and dragging it to the edge. Another option is to right-click on the same app to select "Snap right" or "Snap left" from the menu. Repeat this procedure with the second app as well.

The Power Menu

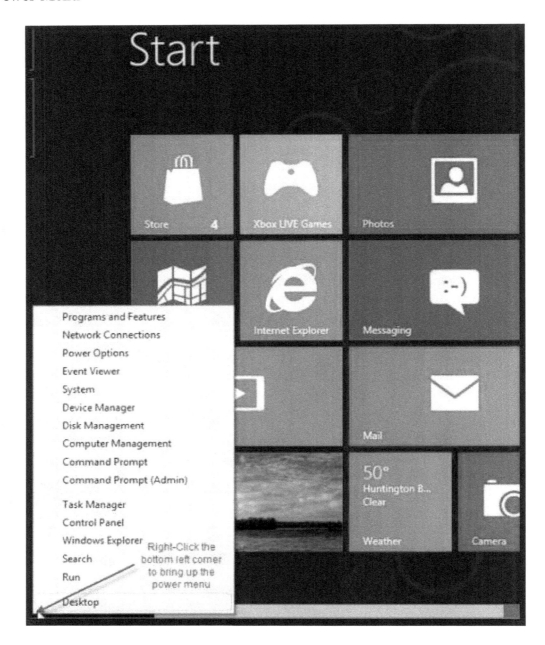

Right-clicking the bottom left corner of the screen will help you see the power menu.

Organizing All the Apps in an Instant

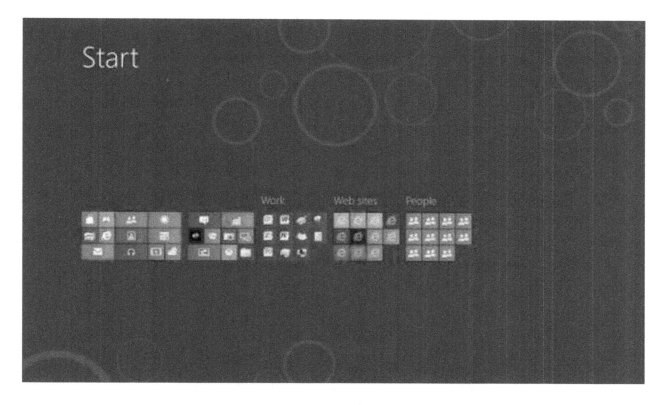

Semantic Zoom is an effective feature to zoom in and zoom out the Start screen, enabling you to organize your apps the way you want.

Pinching your fingers to zoom out will bring you the Semantic Zoom mode. This is used to move files, or create groups of your folders instantly. However, you can use your mouse to enter the same mode.

Vertical scrolling

Simply press and hold Ctrl, and make use of the scrolling wheel on the mouse. This will help you in scrolling in as well as out of the apps of Windows 8.

Hiding Toast Notifications Temporarily

If you want to hide the notifications of some apps for a few hours, you can do this by using the Charm bar. Move the mouse cursor to the right-bottom corner, and click on "Settings", and then "Notifications."

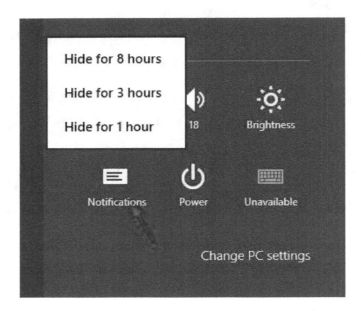

Once done, the icon will reflect the status of the notifications.

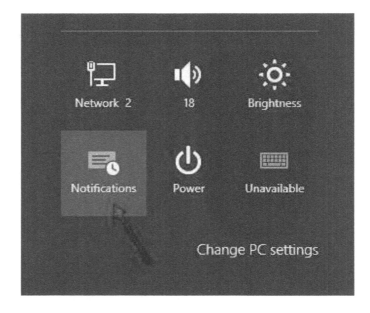

Disabling and Enabling Live Tile Notifications

If you do not want the notifications coming on the top of your live tile, you can disable them with some easy-to-do mouse shortcuts.

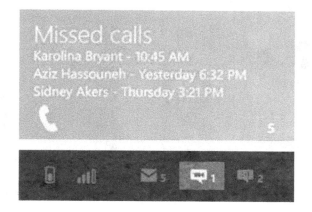

Simply go to your Start screen, right-click the app tile you want to disable notifications from, and select the "Turn live tile off" option.

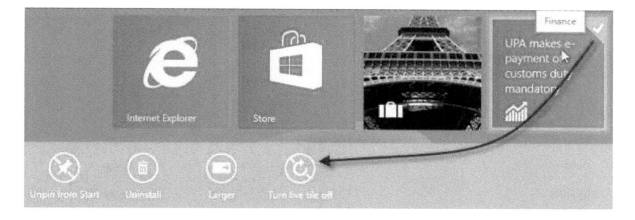

You can enable the same live notifications by selecting the "turn live title on" option.

You may be using various apps at the same time. Getting notifications related to each app can be time-consuming.

So, get rid of them by changing the settings at once, as shown in the image below:

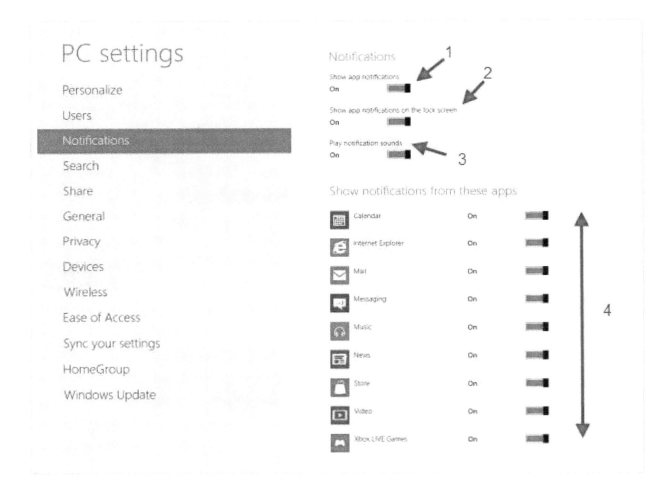

Closing Apps

Click and hold an app from its top edge to move this around your desktop. Now, drag the app to the bottom of this screen. The app will be closed.

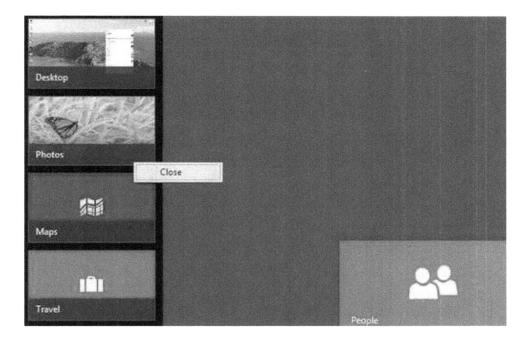

Security and Safety

Windows 8 includes some additional features to enhance security and safety, as explained below:

a. Picture passwords and PINS

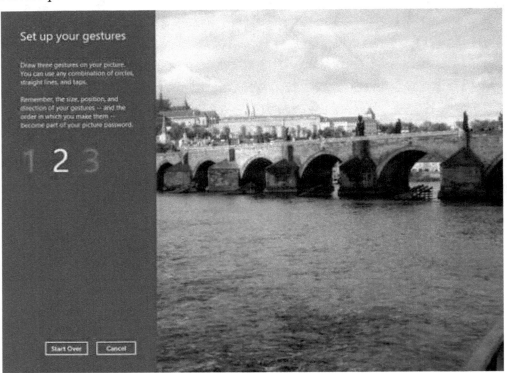

b. Antivirus capabilities in Windows Defender

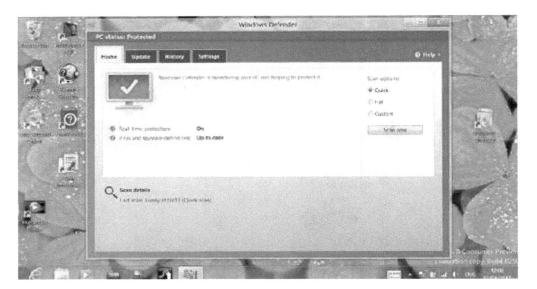

c. SmartScreen Filtering

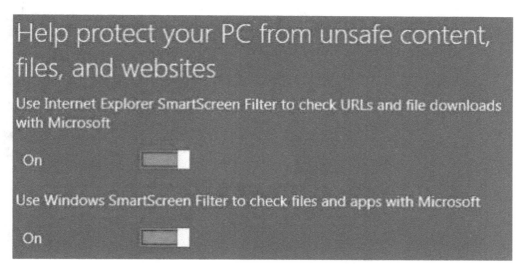

d. Support for the functionality of "Secure Boot"

e. Parental Controls through the Family Safety Software

f. System Recovery

"Windows Store" Apps

Windows 8 has introduced a new application style, known as "Windows Store" apps. These apps are optimized according to the touch screen environments.

In addition, they are in a more specialized form as compared to desktop applications.

Web Browsers

Microsoft has given exceptions to the web browsers of Windows 8, which are categorized as "New experience enabled."

These browsers offer a unique version, running within the shell of "Metro" in terms of an app.

Desktop and Interface

You will see a change in the user interface of Windows 8. This is mainly because it has been designed for various touch screen devices such as, tablet computers.

The user interface of Windows 8 is built on "Metro design" language that also includes a new form of Start Screen, i.e. based on tiled structure.

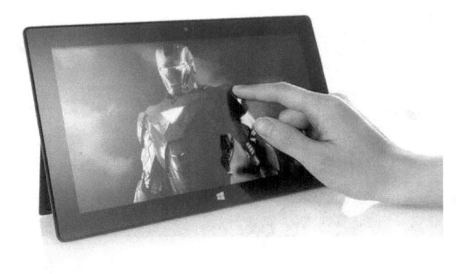

This makes the screen similar to that of Windows Phone.

Secure Boot

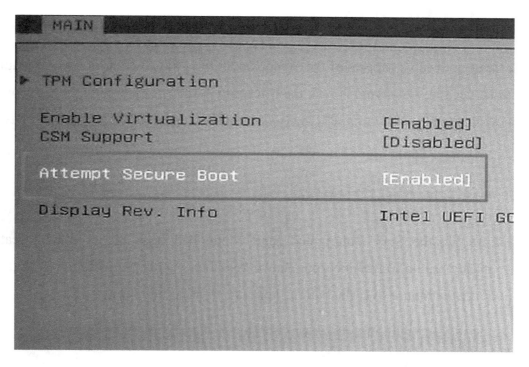

Secure Boot is a feature of "UEFI specification supported by Windows 8. This feature actually uses the "public-key infrastructure" for the verification of the operating system's integrity.

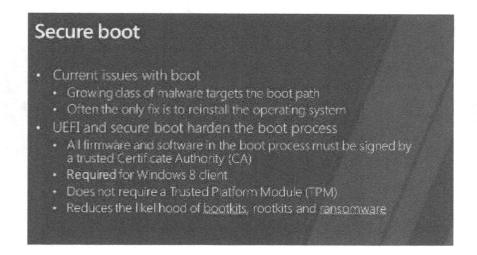

Furthermore, it prevents unauthorized programs, for instance, boot kits. This way, Secure Boot provides security to the functionality of Windows 8.

Removed Features

One of the most noticeable aspects of the Windows 8 OS is the absence of several features that had, with time, become synonymous with the Microsoft Windows enterprise. Earlier you learned about the new features in new OS, but it is also necessary to mention what you don't have on the Windows 8:

Start Button and Start Menu

Since Windows 95, the Start Button and Start Menu had been the prominent features of Windows, but they are no longer incorporated in Windows 8. The Start Button is 'hidden' and you have to hover the mouse over the bottom-left edge to bring into view.

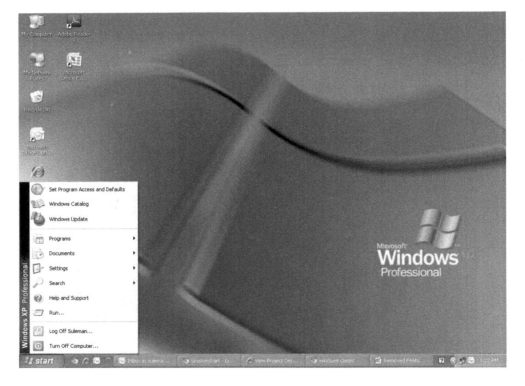

As you already know, the start screen is now based on the Metro style, and while you can search for programs by typing their names, initially it will be a little confusing if you have been heavily accustomed to the conventional Windows desktop.

Windows Aero

Windows Aero was the impressive graphics program on Vista and Windows 7. While it was included in the Window 8 preview version, it has nevertheless been excluded from the commercial release.

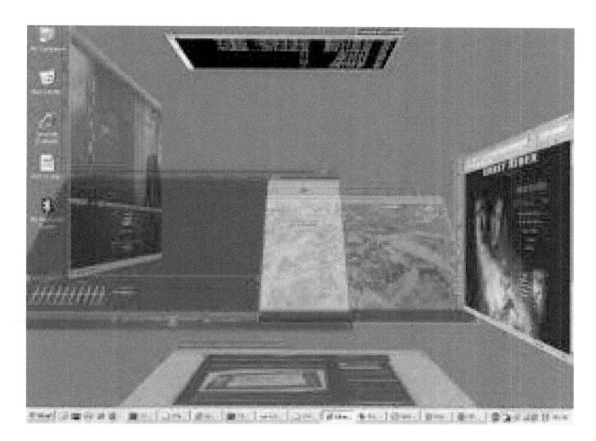

Boot-to-Desktop

The boot-to-desktop feature is also absent. After launching Windows 8, you will directly be taken to the tile-based Metro start screen. Although you can out a 'Show Desktop' shortcut on the startup programs, the screen will appear before the desktop loads.

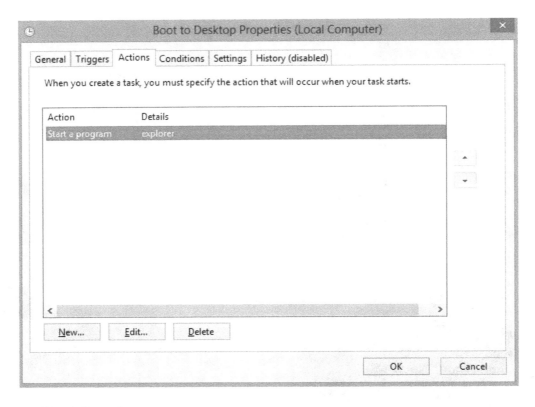

Desktop Notifications

Notifications for updates do not appear on the desktop on the Windows 8. Instead they show up on the login and lock screens. This means that if the PC logs you in automatically, you may not even get to see if any new updates are available.

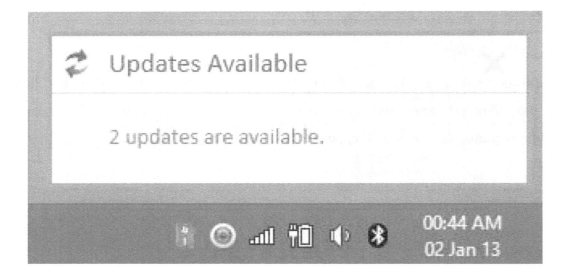

Windows Media Center

Moving on, you will also be missing the Windows Media Center on Windows 8 as it was not being used extensively by Windows owners. You can activate the Windows Media Center via 'Add Features to Windows 8' panel, but you have to pay some money as well.

Previous Versions

The 'Previous Versions' option was built-in in Windows 7, enabling users to restore previous versions of their files from the 'Properties' window.

Along the same lines, Windows 8 also comes without the 'Windows Backup and Restore' feature. 'File History' replaces both these features, but it isn't enabled by default on Windows 8.

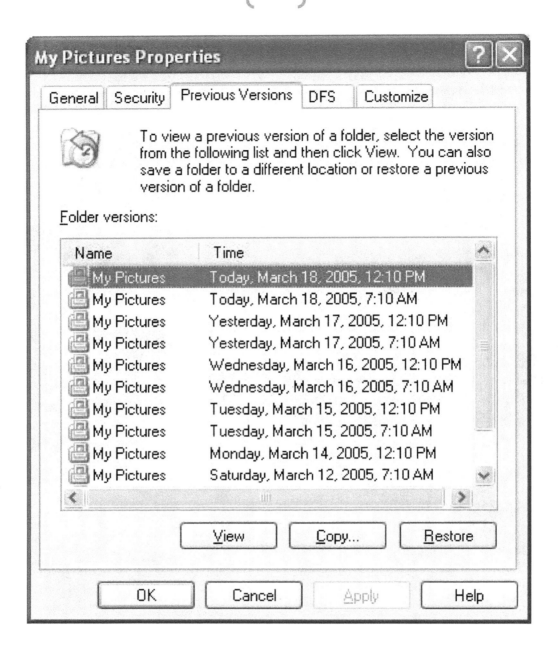

DVD Playback

With the rise of online TV and movie streaming services, fewer people actually watch DVDs on their PCs. Plus, DVD playback doesn't come for free. That is why DVD playback is also included in the list of features removed from Windows 8. Likewise, the Windows DVD Maker is also absent.

Of course, this is not the complete list of what is absent from Windows 8, but these major deprecations are bound to influence the user experience of new customers.

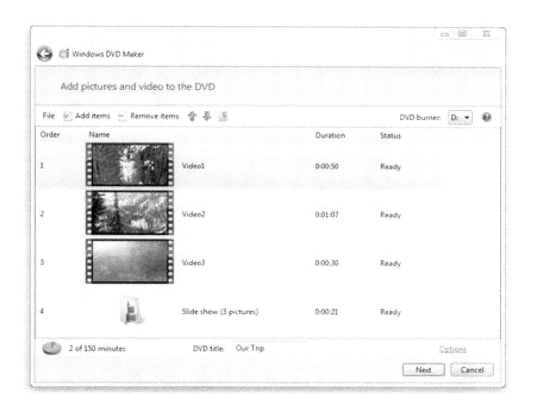

Hardware Requirements

1. PCs

You can easily upgrade to Windows 8 by meeting the following requirements for your PC:

a. -You must have a **processor** of at least 1 GHz

b. -You have a **RAM** of 1 GB (32-bit) or 2 GB (64-bit)

c. -There should **hard disk space** of at least 16 GB (32-bit) or better, 20 GB (64-bit)

d. -You need the Microsoft DirectX 9 graphics with WDDM driver

Note that to access the Window Store, your monitor should have a resolution of at least 1024x768, and to snap the apps, the resolution has to be 1,366x768.

In regards to old hardware, Windows 8 may not have the proper drivers to process them. That is why you are advised to use the Windows 8 Upgrade Assistant to see if your PC is ready for Windows 8.

If the hardware is deemed as inappropriate by Windows Upgrade Assistant, you will have to replace it. You don't necessarily need to purchase new drivers if you had been using Vista before. Vista drivers, for the most part, can run with Windows 8.

2. **Tablets**

When Windows 8 was first launched, Microsoft specifically laid out some instructions for tablets and convertibles.

According to the company, *"A convertible form factor is defined as a standalone device that combines the PC, display and rechargeable power source with a mechanically attached keyboard and pointing device in a single chassis. A convertible can be transformed into a tablet where the attached input devices are hidden or removed leaving the display as the only input mechanism,"*

In addition, some changes were made to these requirements earlier this year which called for tablets to have a minimum resolution on 1024x768. Having said that, here are the major hardware requirements if you want to run Windows 8 on your tablet:

a. **-Storage** of 10 GB

b. **-Camera** of minimum 720p

c. -A DirectX 10 graphics device with WDDM (1.2 or more)

d. -You need an **ambient light sensor** 1-30k lux capable with dynamic range of 5-60k

e. -The tablet should have at least one controller and exposed port for USB 2.0

f. -There should also be connectivity for Wi-Fi and Bluetooth 4.0+LE (low energy)

g. There should be hardware buttons; **Volume-up**, **Volume-down**, **Power**, **Rotation lock**, and **Windows Key**

General requirements include hardware devices like a gyroscope, magnetometer, microphone, and speaker. If your tablet or convertible system has mobile broadband device integration, you will also require assisted GPS radio. If the device has near field communication, visual marks (**Windows Key+Power**).

Tips for Upgradation

When you are finally switching to Windows 8, keep the following tips in mind:

Access the Windows Compatibility Center

You can access the Windows Compatibility link by following this link:

http://www.microsoft.com/en-us/windows/compatibility/win8/CompatCenter/Home?Language=en-US

In this way, you can manually examine each and every hardware and software in your system for Windows 8 compatibility.

Free Up Disk Space

There is a nothing more irritating than a slow PC. While usage will naturally decrease the processing speed of your system, you can follow simple steps like freeing up disk space to make the upgradation slightly faster.

Protect Personal Data

Store all your important personal and work related files (documents, music, pictures) on an external hard drive. However, do ensure that the hard drive doesn't stay connected to the PC at the time of upgradation.

Other things to that will be good to backup include your email and bookmarks. These can easily be backed up online.

Reinstalling Software

You will have to reinstall software programs if you are upgrading from Vista or Windows 7. First, list down all the programs that have to be installed again and then back up their installation files and license keys.

Other programs, like iTunes, require you to either deactivate your license or reauthorize your PC before you can install them again.

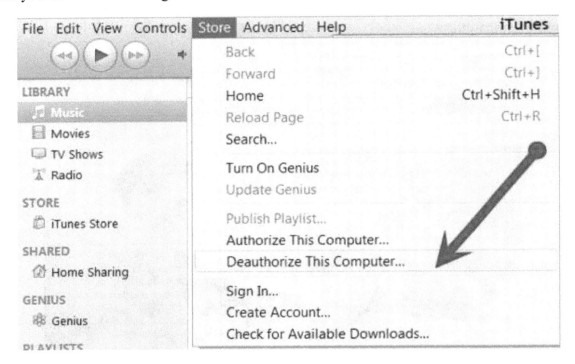

System Backup

If the upgrade doesn't turn out as planned, you may have to go back to your existing OS. That is why you should use system cloning services like Norton Ghost to be on the safe side.

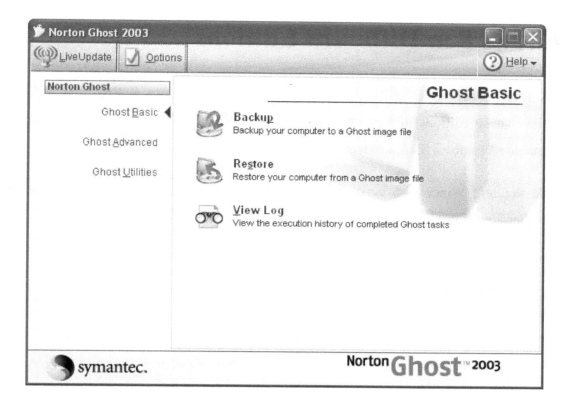

Protect Wi-Fi Password

Finally, it will be an unpleasant experience should you go to all lengths to upgrade your PC and then find not internet connection because you forget your Wi-Fi password!

No matter how basic this advice sounds, you should write down your password before upgrading your PC to ensure that you can immediately begin your internet usage after launching Windows 8.

Windows 8 in Different Editions

This OS is available under editions titled **Windows 8**, **Windows 8 Pro**, and **Windows 8 Enterprise**. These editions in turn have an 'N' version each, which indicates that the edition doesn't include Windows Media Player and other multimedia features.

While the standard Windows 8 version has been discussed extensively in this book, let us run over the other 2 editions:

Windows 8 Pro

If you have used Windows Ultimate or Windows 7 Professional, this edition will suit you. Having the basic functionality of Windows 8, the pro edition is geared towards professional with features like remote desktop access, Encrypting File System, Window Server domain participation, Hyper-V, and BitLocker. With Windows 8 Pro, you will get Window Media Center as a separate software package.

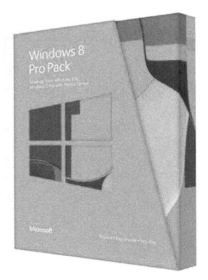

Windows 8 Enterprise

This edition is the same as Windows 8 Pro, but users are enabled to install the Window Media Center add-on.

Apart from the PC versions, **Windows RT** is available (pre-installed) on tablets and devices that run on ARM. While it will have device encryption and touch-based versions of Office 2013, features like domain support and Group Policy cannot be accessed on Windows RT.

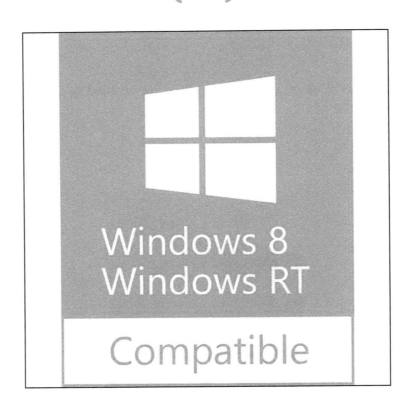

Final Word

Hopefully this guide has proven to be successful in providing you with a detailed insight on Microsoft's latest offering on the OS front. If you have started using computers and Windows 8 is your first OS, you don't even have to bother how Windows 8 is different from its predecessors!

On the other hand, if you are a technology enthusiast, you would have definitely found your knowledge enhanced. While nothing beats hands-on experience, this guide will, in the long run, help you have an all-round view of Windows 8 so that you can use it to its maximum potential.

Good luck!